LUCIA, THE TUGBOAT DOG

By

Ritamary Hanly

Illustrations by

Meghann McCracken

ISBN 0-9711582-0-7

Additional copies of this book are available by mail.
Send $15.00 each (includes tax and postage) to:
Frogpond Books
1710 Beaver Hollow Road
Norristown, PA 19403
(610) 631-0588

Printed in the U.S.A. by
Morris Publishing
3212 East Highway 30
Kearney, NE 68847
1-800-650-7888

DEDICATION

This book is dedicated:

to the thousands of men and women who have served in our Armed Forces, especially in times of battle, and most particularly aboard the Battleship New Jersey.

to the scores of women and men across the country who care for animals in difficulty, both in formal settings as veterinarians and shelter workers, and in informal settings - their own loving homes.

to the children who will read this little labor of love.

Ritamary Hanly

ACKNOWLEDGEMENT

This book was born on November 11, 1999, when I had the honor of sailing on the Tugboat Jupiter as she escorted the Battleship New Jersey up the Delaware River to her birthplace of Philadelphia.

I would like to acknowledge:

Tugboat Jupiter, and the people who were her crew that day, as one of the sources of inspiration for this book.

My husband, Ted Speaker, for his support and patience, and his urging me forward each step of the way.

Meghann McCracken, my illustrator. We met in Miss Gale's dance class, and I quickly was impressed with Meghann's talent in art (she is also a wonderful dancer). Meeting her, and seeing her work, was the final impetus to complete this book.

Sandra Borzillo, who prepared the manuscript for the book. Her assistance was invaluable.

Many family and friends who have listened to the concept of the book, and have encouraged me.

Lucia, our Australian Cattle Dog, whom we adopted from a shelter. Her personality made her a natural to "star" in this little book!

Ritamary Hanly

Greetings from Illustrator, Meghann McCracken . . .

Hello, my name is Meghann McCracken. I am a senior at Methacton High School. That means this year has been a busy one for me. I have concentrated a lot of my efforts on completing my college search. Fortunately, I have been accepted to and am excited to attend Kutztown University as a Communication Design major. As you have most likely concluded, I am interested in art. I spend a majority of my free time working on various art projects. However, I am also involved in many other activities. They include, field hockey, lacrosse, dance lessons, art classes at Moore College, and church youth group. Despite my active extra curricular life, school comes first. I work hard to maintain a good GPA. My favorite classes are AP European history and AP art. I am a part of the community service program at Methacton. Most of my work is done through my church youth group. We go to a local soup kitchen once a month, sponsor out-reach activities and participate in Vacation Bible School.

As far as my family life is concerned, I am the oldest of three children. I have a sister, Erin and a brother, Ryan. My mother and father both work in the school district. Our family is extremely close. We enjoy doing things together, especially taking vacations. My parents are very important to me and I consider them to be my role models. I can always go to either of them when I have any kind of problem. I rely on them for good advice and encouragement. To me they represent all that I would like to achieve in my own life.

This is an exciting time in my life. I look forward to a bright future. I hope some day to be a graphic designer or an illustrator for a well known company. I realize that there will be many challenges ahead, however, I know if I apply what I have learned from school, my family and experience, I will succeed in anything I hope to accomplish.

April 2, 2001

PHIL
RIVER G
JUPITER

It was a cold, damp day in the fall, a few weeks before Thanksgiving. The big, wide river was very dark. At the side of the long dock sat a very old tugboat, the Tugboat Jupiter. A very old tug she was, indeed. Nearly one hundred years ago, she had gone to work in this very same river, the Delaware River, in the City of Philadelphia. Philadelphia was very old too, a city where many important things had happened when America was a very young country.

Tugboat Jupiter sat and sat. She was too old to pull big ships any more. Mainly she sat, and she watched the small boats and big ships and sailboats go up and down the river. Almost every day was the same, and the nights were very lonely for Tugboat Jupiter. She remembered all the years when she had worked, when the nights were not lonely. At night the men who were working on the tug would eat, and sleep, and sometimes sing. The men took turns working in her pilot house, where the big wooden wheel helped steer Tugboat Jupiter up and down the river, pushing a very big ship.

Now, Tugboat Jupiter only went out onto the river for short rides. Sometimes people would pay money to take a ride on her; sometimes people would even have a party on her. Sometimes, she would even do some work, like pulling a small barge, or a sailing ship. Lots of people like tugboats. A group of men and women spent lots of time taking care of Tugboat Jupiter, but she didn't have company every day.

For the past few days, the men and women who cared for her had seemed very excited.

Something was definitely in the air; something good, Tugboat Jupiter thought. But she didn't know what it was. So, she sat, and tried to figure it out.

On this cold day, her crew came to check her engine and all the other important things that helped her run. Tugboat Jupiter was enjoying having them around, when she looked over at the dock. What WAS that thing? Tugboat Jupiter was used to seagulls and other birds. She had even seen a cat or two in her years. But she didn't know what THIS was. Bigger than a cat, with a gray face and black and gray hair on her back. Small brown feet, and a very short tail that looked like part of it was missing. What WAS that?

JUPITER

The little animal looked up at Tugboat Jupiter. "What is THAT?", thought the little dog to herself. The little dog had never seen anything like a tugboat before. She raised her front paw, and sniffed the air. But she still didn't know what that was!

Tugboat Jupiter and the little animal were staring at each other for a very long time. Just when they were going to introduce themselves, Captain Walt, the captain of Tugboat Jupiter, came onto the dock. "A dog!", he said. "What's a dog doing on a dock?" Jack, another crew member, was right behind Walt. "You can't have a dog on a dock or on a boat" Jack said. "They get under foot. They'll trip somebody." "And look", said Captain Walt, "what a very old dog it is!"

"So, that's what it is", said Tugboat Jupiter to herself. "It's a dog" Bigger than a cat, gray face, and tiny little brown feet.

Captain Walt and the rest of the crew came aboard the Tugboat Jupiter. They checked her engines, started her up, cleaned her deck. They were talking a lot, and Tugboat Jupiter could feel that something exciting was coming.

After they had worked for a few hours, Captain Walt and the crew left Tugboat Jupiter for the day. And there, on the side of the dock, was the little dog. "Look at that gray face", said Captain Walt. "I feel sorry for the old dog. It's going to be a cold night." "Dogs don't belong on a dock" said Jack, again.

Frank, another crew member, thought that they should catch the little dog and take her to a shelter for animals. At least she would be warm, and safe, and no one on the dock would trip over her. The rest of the crew agreed, and started walking slowly toward the little dog. The little dog ran. She didn't know who these people were. She wasn't frightened (she's a brave little dog), she just didn't know who these people were.

After a few minutes, the crew, tired from their day of work on Tugboat Jupiter, gave up and went home. The little dog waited until they were gone, and then she came back to the dock. She walked over and sat down next to Tugboat Jupiter. They looked at each other and sighed. Another lonely night. The little dog lay down on the dock next to Tugboat Jupiter, and they both fell fast asleep.

JUPITER

The next day, the sun rose and there they were, still together. The little dog barked to wake up Tugboat Jupiter, and they smiled at each other. The night hadn't been so lonely after all.

A little while later, the crew came back. But, with them today were two people that Tugboat Jupiter had never seen. A man and a woman. Tugboat Jupiter could hear them talking: it was the woman's birthday, a very special birthday. Her name was Emily, and she loved tugboats. For her birthday, her husband, George, had arranged for he and Emily to have a ride on Tugboat Jupiter. When Emily spoke, her words didn't sound exactly like words usually did. She spoke a little bit differently from most people, as though she had come from somewhere far away.

Just then, Emily and George and the crew saw the little dog. "Dogs don't belong on a dock or on a boat" said Jack. "They get under your feet and trip everyone." "And this dog's too old for anything", said Captain Walt. "Oh my", shouted Emily when she saw the little dog. "I haven't seen a dog like that in many, many years, since I was back home in Australia!"

"What?" said Captain Walt. "What do you mean?" "That old dog?" said Jack. Emily laughed as she stooped down to pet the little dog. "That's an Australian Cattle dog. And she's not old. All of them have faces that are gray. My uncle had one of those on his cattle ranch in Australia. Hardest working dog ever. She worked until she was 20 years old. She herded the cattle and guarded the ranch. Lucia was her name."

"Well", said Jack. "A dog's OK on a ranch, but you can't have one on a dock or on a boat. They'll get under your feet and trip everyone."

"Not this kind of dog" said Emily, laughing. "These dogs don't get under anyone's feet. They are so smart and so fast that they can run close behind the cattle, and not get kicked by the cattle's feet. In fact, that's how they herd the cattle - they get their heads down close to the cattle's feet, and bark. They never trip anyone, and they never get kicked."

Emily stooped down, and put out her hand to the little dog. The little dog came very close, and Emily scratched the little dog's head. The little dog's tail wagged so hard that her back wiggled from side to side! "Oh, my", thought the little dog. "that feels so good. I like this lady!" It had been a very long time since anyone had scratched the little dog's head.

"Let's hurry along" said Walt. "We want to get out on the river while we have plenty of daylight." "What about the dog?" asked Emily. "She seems friendly." "Oh no, she's not" said Walt. "Yesterday, we tried to catch her to take her to an animal shelter, where at least she'd be safe. She ran and hid. She's not friendly."

As Emily and George and the crew climbed aboard the Tugboat Jupiter, Emily kept looking toward the little dog. It reminded her of her childhood home. Emily felt a little sad; she wanted to spend some time with the little dog.

As the tugboat pulled away from the dock, the little dog stood watching, one paw up. There was something about Emily that the little dog liked. The little dog watched until she could not see Tugboat Jupiter any longer. Then, she turned and walked slowly away. "I wonder if I'll ever have anyone to scratch my head again", she thought sadly.

Out on the river, the crew were telling Emily and George about something very exciting that was going to happen soon. Tugboat Jupiter listened very carefully. Tugboat Jupiter had heard some talk about this before. Something big was going to happen, but the engines were so loud that Tugboat Jupiter couldn't hear what anyone was saying.

After the ride on the river, Emily and George and the crew went home. When the little dog came back to the dock, she looked for the lady who had scratched her head, but didn't see her anywhere. The little dog curled up and went to sleep on the dock next to Tugboat Jupiter. Funny friends, a big tugboat and a little dog. But friends they were.

For the next few days, the crew spent all day on the tugboat. They checked her engines, and checked them again. They cleaned her deck, and polished the big wooden wheel that steered her They put chairs on the deck, and put flags on the front and back of the tugboat. Tugboat Jupiter was so excited to have company every day! She knew that a very big day was coming soon, though she still didn't know when, or what the big day was about. But every day, she got more excited.

And every night, the little dog came and slept on the dock, next to Tugboat Jupiter.

On one beautiful morning the sun seemed especially bright. "This might be the special day", thought Tugboat Jupiter to herself. Tugboat Jupiter looked down, and, sure enough, she saw lots of cars and people coming onto the dock. "This is it", she smiled, "the special day. Now I'll find out what it's all about."

Lots and lots of people came onto the dock. There were old people and young people, people with flags, people with cameras. Some of the older men and women had uniforms on. "I'll find out very soon what this is all about", thought Tugboat Jupiter. One little boy looked up at Tugboat Jupiter. His mouth fell open. His eyes opened wide. "Grandpa Ted" he said, "look at that big boat. Just like you told me." "Oh no Peter" laughed his grandfather. "That's not the big boat. This is the tugboat that will take us to see the REALLY big boat. And by the way, Peter, really big boats are called ships." "Tell me again, Grandpa Ted" said Peter. "Tell me about the really big boat, I mean ship."

"OK Peter", said Grandpa Ted. "The big ship has a name. It's the Battleship *New Jersey*. She's a very special and proud ship. Very brave people fought to save our country, many times, and the *New Jersey* helped them win the wars." "War is bad, Grandpa Ted" said Peter. Grandpa Ted's face got very sad. "No one likes war, Peter" he said. "But, in that time, years ago, going to war was the only way to save our country. But no one likes war, Peter, and we hope we never have to do it again."

"Why is the big ship coming here today?" asked Peter. Grandpa Ted leaned down and hugged little Peter. "Peter, when the *New Jersey* first went out to sail the ocean and help our country, she left from this very river, this very city. And this tugboat, the Tugboat Jupiter, helped her get into the river. That was a very long time ago. Now, she's coming home on a very special day, when we honor and thank all the men and women who have helped keep our country strong and safe. It's called Veterans Day."

Tugboat Jupiter had been listening, very closely, to Peter and his Grandpa Ted. "So, that's what it's about" thought Tugboat Jupiter. "I remember the *New Jersey*.

She's a great ship. It will be good to see her again." And Tugboat Jupiter got just as excited as all the people were.

Just then, Peter looked up and saw a man in a blue uniform, with lots of bright medals. The man walked over to Grandpa Ted. "Ted", said the man in the uniform, "Ted, remember me? It's been over forty years. How are you?" Grandpa Ted stood up quickly, smiled, and shook hands with the man in uniform, and then they hugged. Peter kept looking around at all the people. He was getting more and more excited. He wanted to get a closer look at the boat that was going to take them out on the river, the Tugboat Jupiter.

Peter took a little walk. He could see the tugboat. He could see big ships sailing on the river. He even saw a funny little dog, sitting on the dock, watching everything and everyone. It was all so big, and so exciting. He liked walking around by himself. He wasn't scared.

In a very short time, Grandpa Ted looked down to take Peter's hand, but little Peter wasn't there. "Where's Peter?" thought Grandpa Ted. "He was right here. I've got to find him, right away." Grandpa Ted looked here

and there, here and there, but couldn't see little Peter. Just then, someone screamed, "Look! Look! That little boy is too close to the edge of the dock. Look!"

All the people turned around, and there was Peter, on the very edge of the dock. Much too close to the cold, deep river. Grandpa Ted and some other people started to run to Peter, but, just then, something ran through the crowd, something small, something very fast. The funny little dog, with her head to the ground, was running toward Peter. Everyone stopped. They didn't know what to think. What would that little dog do? Was she going to hurt Peter? Would she scare him? Would he fall in the river?

In a flash, the little dog ran in front of Peter. She was between Peter and the cold, deep river. She put her head down to the ground, and barked, and moved Peter away from the edge of the dock. Just then, Grandpa Ted and the other people got there. Grandpa Ted picked Peter up and hugged him. And the little dog sat quietly by the edge of the dock.

Captain Walt looked at his watch. "Everyone on board, please" he said. "We're late. We've got to go, right now. The *New Jersey* won't wait for us."

All the people followed Captain Walt, and soon the tugboat was full of people, and getting ready to leave the dock. Peter looked at the dock, and there was the little dog, looking back at him. "Grandpa Ted" said Peter, "can't we take the little dog with us? I like her." Grandpa Ted looked down at the little dog, and smiled. The little dog had saved Peter from falling into the cold dark river.

Grandpa Ted and Peter looked at Captain Walt. "Can she come along, Captain?", said Grandpa Ted. "I think she saved little Peter's life." Captain Walt looked at the other members of the crew, Jack and Frank. They had seen the little dog run along the dock, on her way to save Peter. She didn't trip anyone, or get under anyone's feet. She was very smart, and very fast. In fact, today, she was a hero.

Captain Walt got off the tugboat, and went back onto the dock. "It's OK, little dog", he said, as he knelt down to pet her. "You were a very good dog today. Come for

a ride with us." And Captain Walt picked up the little dog and carried her onto the Tugboat Jupiter. Tugboat Jupiter was very happy to have the little dog along. The little dog made friends with everyone. She ran up to the very front of the tugboat, and sat with Peter and his Grandpa Ted, and they all watched for the big ship, the *New Jersey*.

All along the river bank, hundreds of people were cheering and waving flags to welcome home the *New Jersey*. Grandpa Ted had been very excited about this day, but now all he could think about was that the little dog had saved Peter. Captain Walt and Jack and Frank brought some food to the little dog. She ate a little bit, but she was much too busy watching for the *New Jersey*, and keeping an eye on little Peter, to eat very much.

Soon, the big ship came into view. There were cheers from all the people on the Jupiter, and from all the people along the riverbank. Flags were everywhere. Tugboat Jupiter was so excited to see her old friend the *New Jersey*! Tugboat Jupiter felt just as proud as she had on that day, many years ago, when she had helped the *New Jersey* get out into the deep river. And through all of the excitement, the little dog watched Peter.

For the whole afternoon, Tugboat Jupiter and lots of other boats, big and small, sailed up the river beside the *New Jersey*, welcoming her back to her first home. The sun began to set as the *New Jersey* was guided into her berth, and the wind got very cold, but everyone was having a wonderful time, and everyone was sad when it was time to go home.

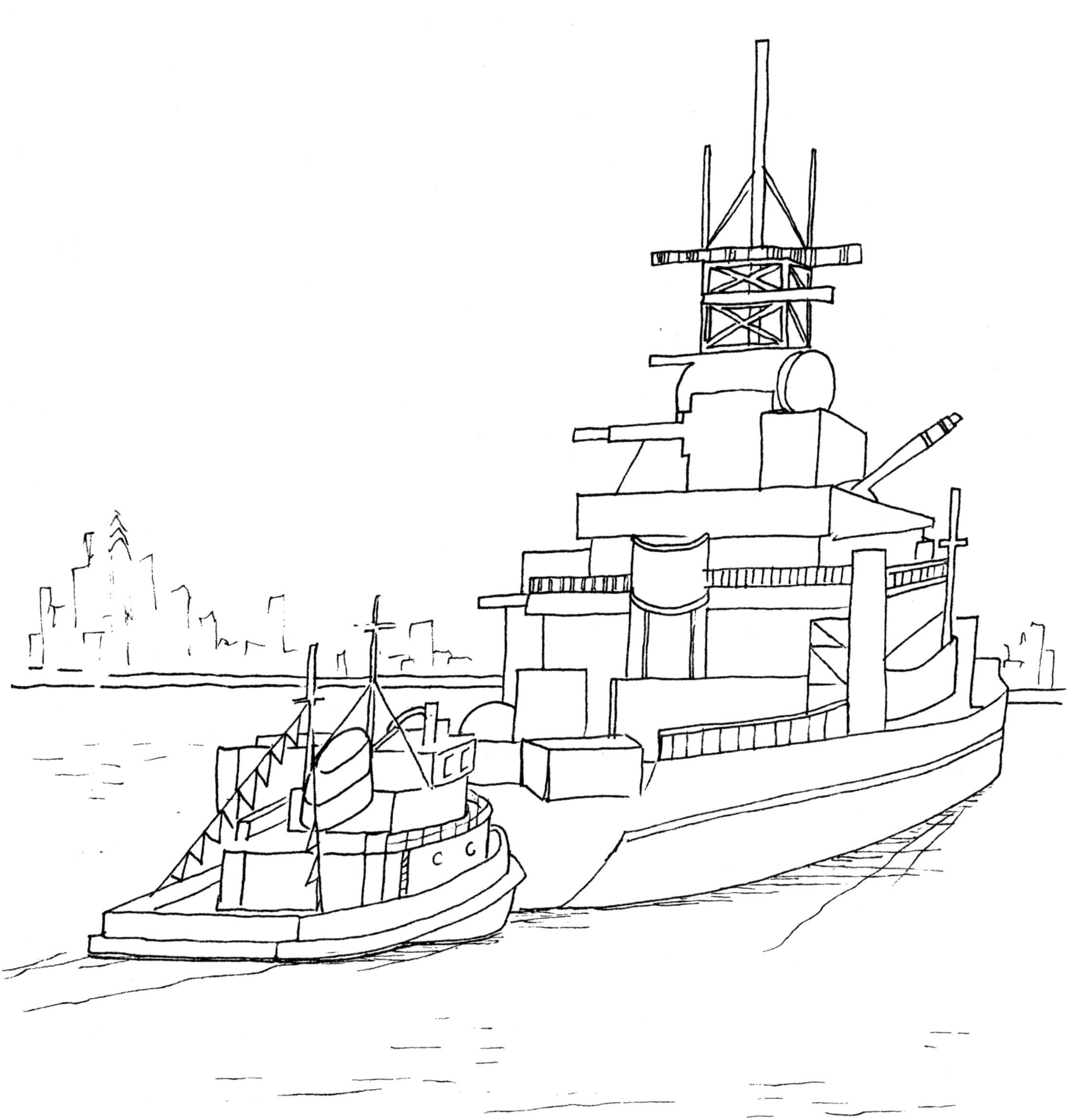
C G

Tugboat Jupiter got back to her dock when it was almost dark. People were bundling up in the cold wind, and hurrying to their cars. Grandpa Ted had little Peter by the hand, but Peter pulled back. "Grandpa Ted", Peter said, "look at the little dog. Where is she going to sleep tonight?" During the day, the little dog had made many friends. "I'll take her home with me", said a man in uniform. "I'd be happy to take her also", said another. The little dog heard all of this. She started to get very excited about having a home, but then she thought of Tugboat Jupiter. The little dog and Tugboat Jupiter had become very good friends. They looked at each other. If the little dog went home with one of the men in uniform, they might never see each other again. The little dog stepped away from the people who wanted to take her home, and walked back to be near Tugboat Jupiter.

Just then, Captain Walt and the crew finished tying Tugboat Jupiter to the dock. Captain Walt had heard the people saying that they wanted to take the little dog home. "Just a minute", he said. "This little dog has been here for a few weeks now. She seems to like being near Tugboat Jupiter. And she showed us today that she knows her way around a dock and around a boat. I'll keep her. She can come here every day with me, and

watch over things, and be with her friend Tugboat Jupiter." Captain Walt bent down, and put his hand under the little dog's chin, and scratched her head. And the little dog's tailed wagged so hard that her back wiggled from side to side!

Tugboat Jupiter and the little dog looked at each other. They would still see each other every day! And the little dog would have a home, and food, and a warm place to sleep, and someone to scratch her head! Oh, this had been a very good day, indeed!

Everyone in the crowd thought it was a very good idea for Captain Walt to take care of the little dog. One person said "Well, then, you must give the little dog a name." Lots of people gave their ideas to Captain Walt - "Name her Tug", said one person. "Jupiter", said another. "Vet" shouted one man. "Jersey" said one woman in uniform.

Captain Walt thought and thought. He remembered Emily, the lady who had said that she had known a dog just like the little dog when she was a small girl, back in Australia. That little dog's name had been "Lucia", and she had been a cattle dog. Captain Walt bent down and

took the little dog's face in his hands. "Lucia", he said, "Lucia." "How do you like that name, little dog?"

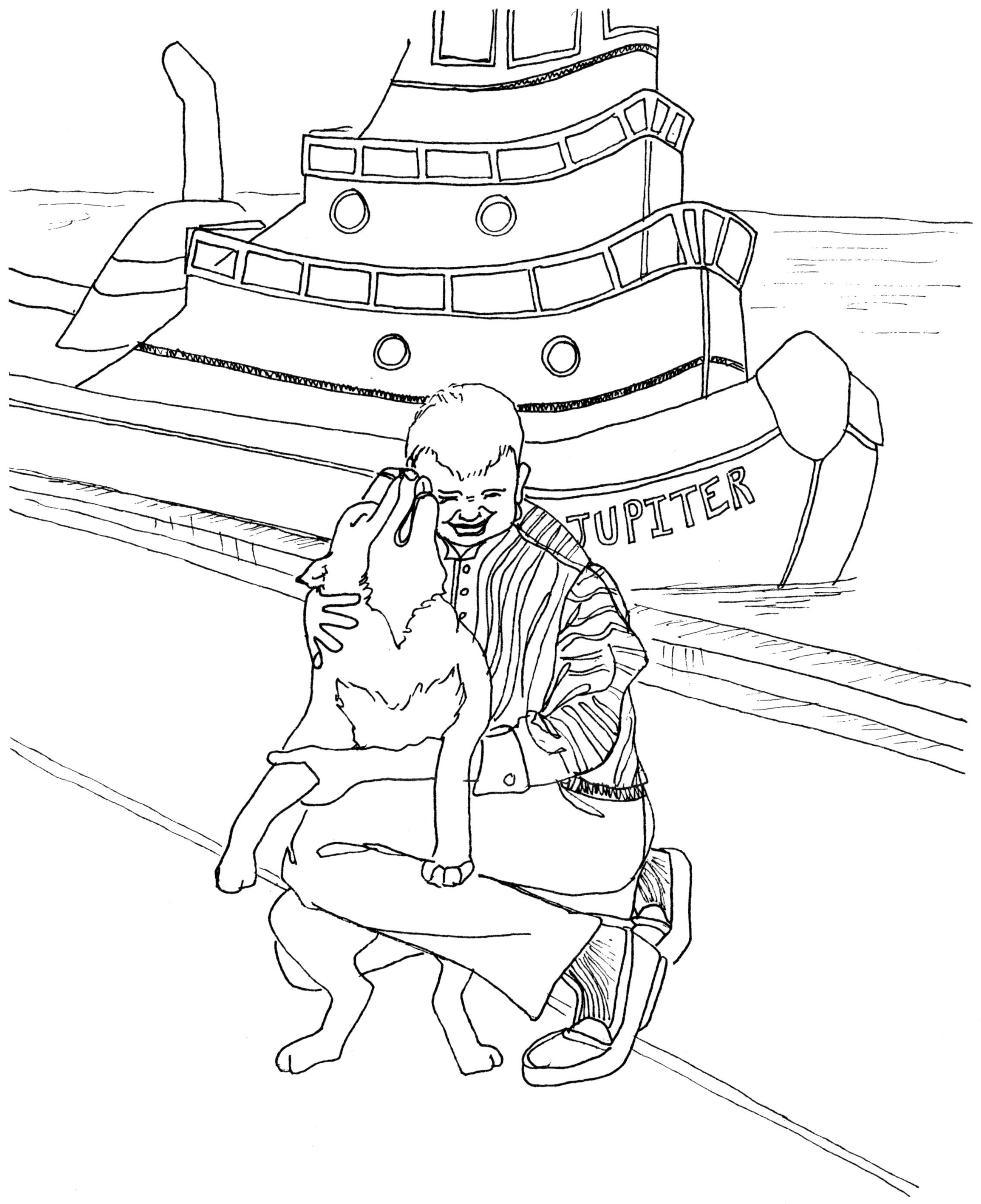
JUPITER

The little dog picked up one paw, snuggled her face into Captain Walt's hands, and gave Captain Walt a kiss on his hand. "Lucia it is", said Captain Walt, "Lucia, the tugboat dog."

All the people cheered and clapped their hands, and shouted "Hooray for Lucia!" Little Peter ran up to the little dog, little Lucia, and gave her a hug and a kiss. Grandpa Ted knelt down and said, "Lucia, you saved Peter's life today. You are a very good, very brave dog, and we are so proud of you."

Lucia looked up at Tugboat Jupiter who was very, very proud, and very, very happy. They smiled at each other. Captain Walt picked up Lucia and gave her a hug. He turned to Tugboat Jupiter and said, "Goodnight, Jupiter. Lucia and I will see you early tomorrow morning."

Tugboat Jupiter watched as Captain Walt and Lucia walked away. Lucia looked back at Tugboat Jupiter and they smiled. We'll see each other in the morning, every morning, they thought. And Captain Walt, Lucia, and Tugboat Jupiter slept very well that night!